Miraculous Magic Tricks
COIN MAGIC

by Mike Lane

Illustrations by David Mostyn

WINDMILL BOOKS

New York

Published in 2012 by Windmill Books, an Imprint of Rosen Publishing
29 East 21st Street, New York, NY 10010

First Edition

Author: Mike Lane
Editors: Patience Coster and Joe Harris
Illustrations: David Mostyn
Design: Tokiko Morishima

Library of Congress Cataloging-in-Publication Data

Lane, Mike.
Coin magic / by Mike Lane.
   p. cm. — (Miraculous magic tricks)
Includes index.
ISBN 978-1-61533-510-7 (library binding) — ISBN 978-1-
4488-6727-1 (pbk.) — ISBN 978-1-4488-6728-8 (6-pack)
1. Coin tricks. I. Title.
GV1559.L345 2012
793.8—dc23
                              2011021764
Printed in China

CPSIA Compliance Information: Batch # AW2102WM: For further information
contact Windmill Books, New York, New York at 1-866-478-0556

SL002048US

CONTENTS

INTRODUCTION

Within these pages you will discover great coin tricks that are easy to do and impressive to watch.

To be a successful magician, you will need to practice the tricks in private before you perform them in front of an audience. An excellent way to practice is in front of a mirror, since you can watch the magic happen before your own eyes.

When performing, you must speak clearly, slowly, and loudly enough for everyone to hear. But never tell the audience what's going to happen.

Remember to "watch your angles." This means being careful about where your spectators are standing or sitting when you are performing. The best place is directly in front of you.

Never tell the secret of how the trick is done. If someone asks, just say: "It's magic!"

THE MAGICIAN'S PLEDGE

I promise not to reveal the secrets of magic to those who are not magicians.

I promise to practice these magic tricks over and over again before attempting to perform them in front of an audience.

I promise to respect my art, the art of magic.

COIN FLIP

ILLUSION
The magician flips a coin from one hand to the other and the coin vanishes.

STICKY TAPE

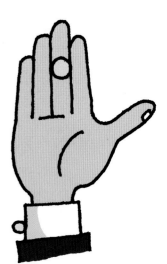

1 Prior to performing the trick, the magician attaches some double-sided adhesive tape to the underside of a small coin. Holding his hand palm up, the magician places the coin midway down his middle finger. The sticky tape will hold the coin in place.

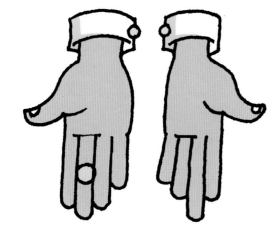

2 To perform the trick, the magician holds out both hands with the palms up, keeping his fingers together.

3 The magician places the hand with the coin across his other hand, to give the illusion that he is transferring or flipping the coin from one hand to the other. The magician keeps the hand with the coin palm down so that he does not expose the coin.

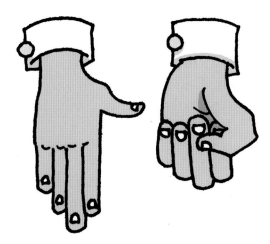

4 He now closes the receiving hand to look as though he is catching and holding the coin.

5 The magician reaches into his pocket with the hand that has the coin in it. He says he is doing this to search for "magic dust." At this point, he drops the coin and tape into his pocket.

6 The magician takes his hand out of his pocket and makes a show of sprinkling invisible magic dust over his other hand, which is clenched and supposedly holds the coin.

MAGIC TIP

COIN TRICKS LIKE THIS ARE EASY TO LEARN, BUT GETTING THE MOVES RIGHT TAKE PRACTICE. PRACTICE MAKES PERFECT, TO "COIN" A PHRASE, BUT IS WORTH IT FOR A MAGICIAN TO IMPRESS HIS SPECTATORS WITH HIS SKILL.

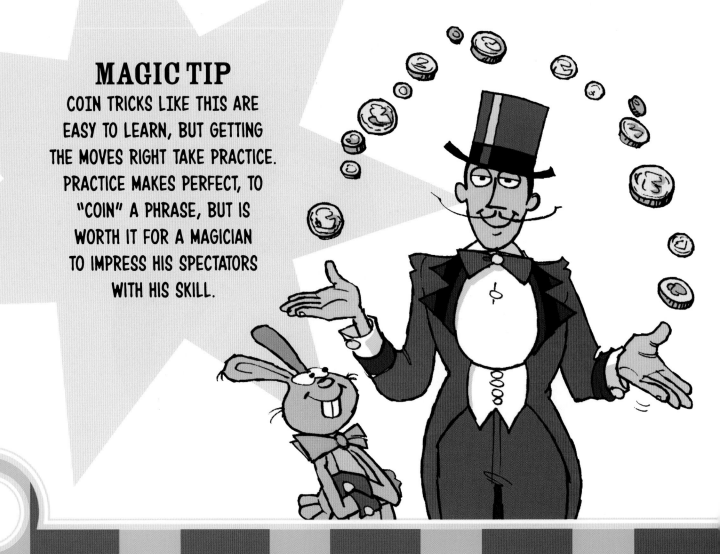

7 The magician opens his clenched hand and— hey presto—the coin has vanished!

8 The magician opens his other hand too, to show that the coin is not hidden there either.

TA-DA!

MYSTERY COIN

1 Holding a coin in his hand, the magician covers it with a bandana. He allows several spectators to feel the coin from above or below, either through the bandana or underneath it.

2 The magician invites as many spectators to feel the coin as he likes. The last spectator to do so has been approached by the magician prior to the performance and is in on the trick. This spectator feels the coin from underneath the bandana, then takes the coin and hides it in his closed hand.

3 The magician whisks away the bandana, showing that the coin has gone. He holds up his empty hand for all to see and allows the spectators to examine the bandana.

4 The magician covers his empty hand with the bandana and invites the same spectators to feel that there is no coin there.

5 When it comes to the turn of the last spectator (the one with the coin), he or she places the coin in the magician's hand underneath the bandana.

6 The magician whisks away the bandana to show that the coin is mysteriously back in his hand.

COIN LEAP

1 Prior to the trick, the magician sews a coin into the corner of a bandana. This is called the "prepared bandana."

2 The magician gives a coin to the spectator and asks him to write his initials on it using a marker. This coin must be identical to the one that has been sewn into the bandana.

3 The magician now takes the marked coin from the spectator and, with the same hand, picks up the prepared bandana by the corner into which the coin has been sewn.

4 From underneath, the magician draws the sewn-in coin corner into the middle of the bandana, using the hand that is also holding the marked coin. Not knowing that a coin has been sewn into the bandana, the spectator believes that the sewn-in coin is his marked coin.

5 The magician puts down the prepared bandana and picks up a second bandana. He places his hand under it with the marked coin in the middle. He then takes hold of the coin and bandana from above.

6 With his other hand now empty, the magician picks up the prepared bandana again by the coin.

7 The magician shakes out the prepared bandana by a corner to show that the coin has vanished. He then shakes out the second bandana to reveal that the spectator's marked coin has leapt into it.

COIN FROM PAPER

1 Prior to the trick, the magician hides a coin behind the bottom righthand corner of a bill. He keeps the coin in place with his thumb, with his four fingers held in front of the bill.

2 To perform the trick, the magician holds up the bill and folds it in half from left to right.

3 He then folds it in half again, being sure to keep the coin hidden.

4 The magician folds the bill a third time toward himself from top to bottom, still being sure to hide the coin, which is now in the middle of the folded bill.

5 The magician holds his left hand, palm up, under his right hand. He drops the coin out of the bill into his left hand.

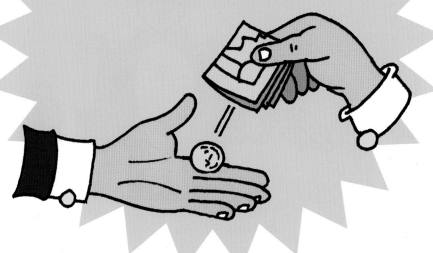

COIN RUB

ILLUSION
The magician shows that both hands are completely empty, front and back. The magician rubs his hands together and a coin appears.

1 For this trick, the magician needs to wear a long-sleeved shirt or jacket. Prior to the trick, the magician places a coin in the crease of his left elbow on top of the jacket.

2 The magician starts the trick by holding both his arms bent upward slightly.

3 The magician opens his right hand to show the spectator that it is empty.

4 With his right hand, the magician pulls slightly on his left sleeve, stating: "There is nothing up my sleeve." While doing this, the magician takes the coin hidden in the crease of his jacket and hides it in his right hand.

5 The magician opens his left hand to show the spectator that it is empty.

6 With his left hand, the magician pulls slightly on his right sleeve stating: "There is nothing up this sleeve either."

7 The magician slowly rubs both his hands together.

PENNY, NICKEL

ILLUSION

A spectator places a coin in one hand and a coin of a different value in his other hand. He holds his hands behind his back, making it impossible for the magician to know which coin is in each. Yet the magician can tell which coin is in each hand.

1 The magician gives a penny and a nickel to the spectator and asks him to place his hands behind his back.

2 The magician asks the spectator to place a coin in each hand.

3 Once that is done, he asks the spectator to hold his hands in front of him in fists.

4 The magician points to one of the hands and asks the spectator to multiply the value of that coin by 16. The spectator must let the magician know as soon as he has the answer but he must not say it out loud.

5 Now the magician points to the other hand and asks the spectator to do the same sum with the other coin.

6 The hand that the spectator figured out the answer for in less time will be the penny, because it is much easier to multiply 16 by 1 than 16 by 5.

$16 \times 1 = 16$

$16 \times 5 = ??!!!?80$

7 The magician now tells the spectator which coin is in each hand.

A COOL COIN TRICK

ILLUSION

The magician has six similar coins and several spectators. One of the spectators marks a coin while the magician is out of the room. The magician returns to the room and picks the marked coin without looking at it.

1 The magician shows some spectators six coins, a marker, and a hat.

2 The magician explains that he will leave the room and that while he is outside a spectator should mark one of the coins.

3 When this is done, the spectator must hold that coin in her fisted hand and concentrate on it by bringing her fist up to her head. The coin should then be given to the other spectators to do the same.

4 Once the spectators have done this, they should place all the coins in the hat.

5 The magician returns to the room, reaches into the hat without looking, and feels each coin.

6 He draws out the marked coin. The coin that is warm is the coin that was held by the spectators, and is therefore the marked coin.

SWEATING COIN

ILLUSION
A coin is handed around for inspection. Sweat begins to drip from it when it is returned to the magician.

1 The magician asks the spectators to examine a coin (this trick works best with a large coin).

2 Hidden in the magician's hand is a small piece of tissue that is scrunched up and dampened with water.

3 When the magician takes the coin back from the spectators he hides the tissue behind it.

4 The magician explains that by squeezing the coin he can make it sweat.

5 The magician now starts to squeeze the coin, while also squeezing the tissue against the back of the coin. This causes water to drip from the tissue and creates the appearance that sweat is dripping from the coin.

COIN CATCH

1 This trick requires practice. Start by bending your right arm (or left arm, if you are left-handed) with the palm of your hand facing forward, until the back of your hand touches your shoulder. The elbow should be pointing forward. Your arm does not need to be perfectly straight, but keep it as level as you can.

2 With the other hand, place a stack of coins on your elbow.

30

3 When ready, flip your arm down quickly and catch the coins with the same hand.

4 Start with just one coin. Slowly build on this by adding more coins and stacking them up.

5 As you get better at the trick, add more coins to the stack. With practice, this trick can be done with stacks of coins on both arms for maximum effect!

FURTHER READING

Barnhart, Norm. *Amazing Magic Tricks.*
    Mankato, MN: Capstone Press, 2008.
Cassidy, John and Michael Stroud. *Klutz Book
    of Magic.* Palo Alto, CA: Klutz Press, 2006.
Charney, Steve. *Awesome Coin Tricks.*
    Mankato, MN: Capstone Press, 2011.
Klingel, Cynthia. *Magic Tricks.* Mankato, MN:
    Compass Point Books, 2002.
Longe, Bob. *Classic Magic Tricks.* New York,
    NY: Metro Books, 2002.

WEB SITES

For Web resources related to
the subject of this book, go to:
www.windmillbooks.com/weblinks
and select this book's title.

GLOSSARY

bandana (ban-DA-nah) Colorful
    cloth worn on the head.
clenched (KLENCHD) Tightly closed.
hey presto (HAY PRES-toh) What
    magicians say when they mean
    "suddenly—as if by magic!"
illusion (ih-LOO-shun) An image that
    you see but is not what it seems to be.
magic dust (MA-jik DUST) Imaginary
    powder used by magicians
    to perform their tricks.
maximum effect (MAX-sih-mum
    ih-FEKT) The best possible result.

INDEX